THE IDENTITY WE KEEP SECRET...

BY: Josh Nedrick

Copyright © 2025 by Josh Nedrick

All rights reserved. No part of this book may be used or reproduced in any form whatsoever without written permission except in the case of brief quotations in critical articles or reviews.

Printed in the United States of America and or Canada

For more information or to book an event, contact :
info@cojbokz.com
Cover design by Josh Nedrick

ISBN - Paperback: 978-1-998120-77-2

CHAPTER 1

The Roots Beneath Our Feet

"Before the chains, there was the crown."

Before the world tried to box us in, silence our voices, or sell our stories for a profit, we were rooted in greatness. Our beginnings didn't start on the auction block or in the margins of someone else's history book. They began long before that—in the womb of civilization itself. The lands of Africa, lush with life and wisdom, birthed empires, languages, medicine, and art long before colonizers could even draw maps.

We are the descendants of dynasties. Not myths, but movements. Not fairy tales, but **fact**.

The Nile flowed past libraries in Timbuktu. Griots passed down oral legacies that stretched further than the longest scrolls in ancient Europe. Mathematics, astronomy, and architecture were not borrowed knowledge—they were ours first. And yet, when history was rewritten, it erased those truths. Or tried to. But soil doesn't forget the seeds it once held. And neither do we.

The blood that runs through our veins carries stories of builders, rulers, thinkers, and warriors. Not just of survival, but of sovereignty. These were not people content to merely exist—they created worlds. They commanded land and legacy with wisdom that came from being deeply in tune with the earth, the spirit, and the stars above.

So when we speak of **ancestry**, we're not just talking about where we came from—we're acknowledging what we come *with*. A rich inheritance. Not of gold and jewels, but of purpose, power, and potential.

And that's what they tried to break.

When colonizers arrived, they saw the wealth, not just in material, but in mind and spirit. And they feared it. So they took. They stole land, stole people, stole names, and tried to bury the truth. They broke the drums but not the rhythm. They severed tongues but not the language that lived in the body. They renamed us, beat us, dehumanized us—trying to make us forget. But forgetting was never an option.

Because even if they disrupted the story, they couldn't erase the roots.

And now those roots are rising. Again.

We walk with a knowing—an ancestral memory—that we are not defined by our trauma. We are shaped by it, yes, but not confined to it. What our ancestors began, we carry. Their battles, their brilliance, their unfinished dreams—those live on in us.

So as we stand here today, in a world that still tries to reduce us to tropes and trends, we start this journey by looking back—not to dwell, but to remember. Because what's remembered can be reclaimed. And what's reclaimed can be reborn

CHAPTER 2

The Mirror And The Myth

"To know who you are, you must first confront the reflection they gave you."

When a child is born into this world, they don't arrive with shame or limitation. They come in whole, brilliant, and untouched by the lies of society. But the moment that child looks into the mirror of the world, the distortion begins.

For us—for Black boys and Black girls—the mirror ain't always been kind.

From a young age, we are fed images that don't reflect our truth. Television, textbooks, magazines, movies, even classrooms—all of them participate in constructing a version of our identity shaped by fear, fetish, and fiction.

We are either criminalized or commodified.
Feared or fetishized.
We're rarely shown as full human beings.

The curve of a Black woman's hips becomes hypersexualized. The depth of her voice is deemed "aggressive." The beauty of her natural hair becomes "unprofessional." Meanwhile, her style is stolen, her slang co-opted, her image copied without credit. The Black man is no different, cast either as a threat or a joke. A body without a soul. Muscles without intellect. A moment, but never a movement.

This is not accidental.

This is designed because if they can control how we see ourselves, they can control how we move. If we believe we are less, we will accept less. If we accept less, they keep power.

But here's the thing about mirrors: they can crack.

And when they do, so do the lies.

We are not the sum of stereotypes.

We are not the headlines they use to define us.

We are not "too loud," "too much," or "too other."

We are the *blueprint*.

We are the *influence* behind what they praise, the culture behind what they consume, and the trendsetters for what they call "cool." But beyond the aesthetic, we are architects of innovation. Of love. Of resilience.

Look deeper into our mirror and you'll see:
We're not just what the world perceives—we are what the world needs.

Because the truth is, our identities stretch far beyond this generation's understanding. We carry multiple selves, forged across continents and time. Royal blood, rebel fire, divine energy—all living in one skin. Our culture isn't just performative—it's preservative. Every time we wear our hair in braids, speak our language,cook our food, or name our children in honor of those who came before, we are practicing revolution.

To unlearn the myth, we must study the truth.

And the truth is:

We are **soft and strong.**

Complex and clear.

Wounded and winning.

We are in the middle of the storm and the calm that follows.

We are the definition of balance—grace under pressure, joy through pain, dignity through the disrespect.

When we truly see ourselves, not through their lens, but through the eyes of our ancestors, we remember:

We were never the problem.

We were the answer all along.

So the question is no longer:

"How do they see us?"

It's: How do we choose to see ourselves?

When we look in the mirror now, we see royalty.

We see visionaries.

We see legacy in the making.

And with that vision, we rise!

CHAPTER 3

The Chains And The Change

"They tried to break us, but we bent into something unshakable."

To understand where we're headed, we gotta face what we've been through.

Not for pity. Not for permission. But for **perspective**.

Because our struggle ain't just a wound—it's a **weapon**.

It's the hammer we used to break open cages.

It's the fire that taught us how to shine even in the dark.

Let's be clear: **they did everything in their power to break us.**

They dragged us from the shores of our homelands.

Shackled our bodies in ships with no light, no air, no dignity.

Families torn, names stolen, languages erased.

And then, once here, we were bought and sold like property.

Whipped for reading. Lynched for looking. Shot for existing.

Made to feel like we were subhuman. Made to believe our only value came from labor, not love.

But pain births power.

And what they didn't understand was that every scar they carved into our history only made us harder to erase.

We spoke of freedom in languages they couldn't understand.

We danced joy into our bodies even when joy was outlawed.

We braided maps into our children's hair.

We passed down knowledge through stories, songs, and scripture.

We turned sorrow into spirituals.

We turned chains into rhythms.

We turned fields into forums of survival.

And even after so-called emancipation, the struggle just evolved.

Jim Crow laws, redlining, underfunded schools, prison pipelines, police brutality—all modern-day shackles meant to keep us in the same place, mentally and physically.

But somehow, **we kept moving**.

We marched. We sat in. We stood up. We rose.

Every generation passed the torch—sometimes with bruised hands—but always with unshaken faith.

They told us we were criminals.
We became judges.

They told us we were dumb.
We became scholars, doctors, and engineers.

They told us we were worthless.
We became artists who defined global culture.

They told us we were just bodies.
We became **beacons.**

The chains were real—but so was the **change.**

Because every time they tried to suppress us, we reinvented ourselves.
They said we couldn't have education—we built HBCUs.
They said we couldn't vote—we organized movements.
They said we'd never be equal—we became presidents, poets, professors, and pioneers.

What makes us different is this:

We've mastered the art of alchemy.

Turning pain into purpose.

Turning trauma into testimony.

Turning broken systems into stepping stones.

But don't get it twisted—we're still healing.

Generational wounds don't fade overnight.

We still carry the echoes of trauma in our bones, the silence of our ancestors in our sleep.

We still watch our people die on camera and feel our hearts break publicly.

We still walk into rooms and shrink, second-guessing our worth.

Still get followed in stores, still questioned in classrooms, still stereotyped in boardrooms.

But here's the shift:

Now we know better.

And when you know better, you build better.

This generation? We ain't asking no more.

We're demanding.

We're designing new spaces.

We're developing our own platforms.

We're deciding our own futures.

And it all started with the ones who endured the worst of the chains, so we could taste even a little of the change.

So we honor them—not with pity, but with power.

We honor them by becoming the free people they dreamed of when freedom was just a whisper.

Because we are not just survivors—we are **strategists.**

We are not victims—we are **visionaries.**

The chains were heavy.

But the change?

It's unstoppable.

CHAPTER 4

The Rise Within The Noise

"We were never background. We are the main event."

Even in the face of chains, oppression, and erasure, we rose.
We rose when it wasn't quiet.
We rose while the world was screaming at us to sit down, shut up, blend in, be less.
But the thing about greatness? It doesn't ask permission to speak—it just shows up. Loud, brilliant, undeniable.

So while the noise tried to drown us, we became **the sound**.

Let's talk about *culture*.
Black culture doesn't *influence* the world—it **moves** it. Period.

From the drumbeats of West Africa to the trap beats of Atlanta, our rhythm is the planet's pulse.
Hip hop ain't just music—it's a billion-dollar blueprint. Born from poverty, raised in resistance, and now runnin' the globe.

Jazz. Soul. Blues. Funk. Reggae. Dancehall. Afrobeats.

We gave the world soundtracks to liberation, to love, to life.

And when they told us we were just entertainers?

We flipped it.

Turned the stage into a statement.

Turned lyrics into lessons.

Turned style into scripture.

From MJ moonwalking to Beyoncé shutting down stadiums, from Tupac's poetry to Kendrick's Pulitzer, we've been proving we ain't just rhythm—we're revolution.

But we didn't stop at the mic. Nah.

We took over the **screens** as well.

Sidney Poitier walked so Denzel could run.

Viola, Lupita, Zendaya—Black women redefining beauty and brilliance.

Jordan Peele flipping horror into commentary.

Issa Rae is creating stories where we're not the sidekick—we're the story.

We created Wakanda from our wildest dreams and proved that Black imagination can break box offices.

But don't get it twisted. We ain't just out here entertaining.
We **building**. We **owning**.
We **bossed up**.

We went from being the talent to becoming the **label**.
From rocking brands to **starting** them.
FUBU wasn't just fashion—for us, by us was a mission.
Telfar, Off-White, Fear of God—Black luxury is the new standard.
And in tech? In finance? In law?
Yeah, we're out here too.

From Madame C.J. Walker to Rihanna's empire.
From Robert F. Smith to Daymond John.
From HBCU grads building apps to Black women leading hedge funds—
We've made it clear: **we are not just creatives. We are creators of capital.**

And the wild part?

We've been doing this.

Even when doors were locked, we made keys.

Even when tables weren't offered, we built our own.

Pop-up shops, barbershops, beauty salons, poetry slams, open mics—those were our boardrooms.

Those were our think tanks.

What they called "the hustle"—we knew was brilliance in motion.

Because our rise didn't come from ease. It came from necessity.

We had to be twice as good with half the resources.

Had to work harder, speak softer, smile more, just to be seen.

But now?

Now we speak boldly. Walk proudly. Take up space *fully*.

We're not waiting to be discovered.

We're **defining ourselves**.

Writing our own scripts, owning our narratives, putting our names in rooms where they once left us off the list.

We still have hurdles. Still got ceilings.

But the difference now?

We got wings.

And we owe it to the ancestors who danced in chains.

To the grandmothers who built businesses out of kitchens.

To the fathers who worked three jobs so we could dream.

To the youth who remix the struggle into success every day.

They tried to bury us in noise.

But all they did was amplify our signal.

We rose in every lane—

Not to prove our worth. But to remind them, we never stopped being worthy.

CHAPTER 5

The Reclamation

"We didn't lose our power—we just had to remember where we put it."

Reclamation ain't just a return—it's a revolution.

It's not about nostalgia or going backwards.

It's about recognizing what was taken, what was twisted, and choosing—*intentionally*—to claim it back, reshape it, and make it ours again.

Because real talk? We've been robbed.

Not just of resources, but of **identity**.

They gave us new names, fed us lies, buried our languages, painted over our gods, and told us who we were supposed to be.

They turned our heritage into Halloween costumes.

Our hairstyles into "unprofessional."

Our dialects into "ghetto."

Our anger into "threat."

Our style into "urban wear."

And our history into footnotes.

But here's the truth: we remember.

Not always with clarity, but with **calling**.

There's something spiritual in our bones, something sacred in our DNA.

Something that refuses to die.

Something that says:

> "This ain't all of me. There's more. There's deeper. There's divine."

So we start taking it back. Piece by piece.

We drop the word "dread" and call them **locks**.

Because there's *nothing* dreadful about our hair growing the way it was designed to.

Our coils, our curls, our crowns—they ain't mistakes, they're **monuments**.

Living, breathing art pieces that speak to ancestry, style, and strength.

We reclaim our **names**.

Not just the ones they renamed us with, but the ones our people carried with pride.

We're naming our babies with intention now—after tribes, after queens, after warriors, after languages stolen but never silenced.

We reclaim our **languages**—Patois, Yoruba, Twi, Krio, Swahili, AAVE—all of it.
The way we talk ain't broken English—it's **survival code**.
Rhythmic. Real. Rooted in resilience.
They tried to beat the dialect out of our tongues, but it stayed in our spirit.

We reclaim our **spirituality**, too.
Nah, we ain't all tied to pews and pulpits.
Some of us light candles for ancestors, some of us drum with intention, some of us burn sage to cleanse spaces.
Before religion was colonized, our people already walked with the divine.
We knew how to speak to the stars, honor the moon, and pour libations to those who came before us.
That ain't superstition—that's *sacred*.

We reclaim our **histories**.

No longer depending on the watered-down textbooks to tell our tales.

We doing our own research. Reading between the lines. Writing the missing chapters.

From the pyramids of Kush to the Maroons of Jamaica, from the Zulu Kingdom to the freedom fighters in the Bronx—

We're telling the *full* story now. Loud and proud.

We reclaim our **bodies,** too.

No longer letting the media define beauty through Eurocentric filters.

Thick thighs, broad noses, deep skin, full lips—every feature they mocked, we now **magnify**.

We ain't asking to be accepted. We *are* the standard.

Reclamation is an act of war *and* worship.

It's rebellious self-love.

It's a refusal to apologize for our power.

It's walking into spaces that weren't built for us and making them ours.

It's knowing that just being ourselves is an act of **defiance** in a system that tried to erase us.

But don't get it twisted—this ain't about revenge.
This is about **remembrance**.
About taking the shattered pieces and rebuilding the mosaic.
About saying: "This is mine. This was *always* mine. And I'm never letting it go again."

And now?
We're passing that fire down.
To the next generation.
Letting them know they don't have to search for their worth—it's already in them.

We don't just come from pain.
We come from **power**.
We come from **purpose**.
And now we walking like we know that truth. Talking like it.
Creating like it. Dressing like it. Living like it.

Because when we reclaim who we are,
We reclaim **what we're meant to become!**

CHAPTER 6

From Legacy To Leadership

"We are the prayers of our ancestors — now it's our turn to lead."

Legacy don't end with memory.

It continues in **movement**.

And leadership? It ain't always suits and stages.

Sometimes, it's quiet. Sometimes it's loud.

But always, it's rooted in love, vision, and a responsibility to those coming next.

We stand today not just as individuals, but as **descendants of greatness**.

We are the result of generations who refused to fold.

Every freedom we flex today came from the sacrifice of those who couldn't.

So we don't just inherit stories — we inherit **missions**.

And the mission now?

To not just survive. Not just inspire.

But to **lead**.

To shift systems.

To build tables, not just sit at them.
To break cycles and build bridges.

We ain't just tryna make history — we tryna **shape the future.**

Let's talk **legacy** first.

Legacy ain't just land or bank accounts.
It's culture.
It's confidence.
It's creating space for our people to be seen, heard, and safe.
It's giving the next gen what we wish we had growing up — guidance, truth, access, protection, power.

Legacy is Big Mama's stories around the table.
It's those unspoken looks from elders that say, "Keep goin', baby."
It's traditions passed down, even when the world told us to forget.
It's the torch handed off in silence, but felt in every step we take.

Now let's flip it — **leadership**.

Our leadership doesn't always look like the textbook version. We lead from the block to the boardroom, from the classroom to the culture.

The single mother holding it down and raising visionaries?
That's leadership.

The OG who turned their pain into mentorship for the youth?
That's leadership.

The young queen launching a hair care line out of her dorm room?
Leadership.

The teacher in an underfunded school pouring belief into every kid?
Major leadership.

The poet spitting bars about revolution on an open mic?
Still leadership.

We lead by example. By truth. By showing what's possible when resilience meets purpose.

But here's where it gets deeper:
We don't just lead for the applause — we lead for the **impact**.

It ain't enough to rise alone.
We build ladders, not pedestals.
We teach what we learn.
We leave the door open behind us.
Because we know what it's like to start from locked gates and blocked roads.

Our role now is to **plant seeds** we might never see grow.
To build institutions. Fund futures. Protect dreams.

Whether we are CEOs or community organizers, creators or coders, we hold the pen now.
And leadership means writing a story that uplifts more than just *us*.

It means turning our platforms into pulpits.
Our pain into policy.

Our vision into structure.

And our communities into legacies that last.

And yo, the youth? They watching.

Not just what we say, but how we live.

So we gotta be intentional.

Be the blueprint and the builder.

Be the proof that royalty still runs in our veins.

Be the ones who protect our culture while evolving it.

Be the ones who turn trauma into tools and history into a handbook for elevation.

It's on us to teach them:

You ain't just a product of your environment — you're a **producer of the future.**

You ain't waiting on permission — you're walking in purpose.

You don't need to *fit in* — you were born to **stand out**.

And when we lead like that?

We honor every ancestor that dared to dream of a day when

we could move this freely, speak this loudly, and lead this boldly.

We become the bridge between **what was** and **what's next**.

Acknowledgment

I want to sincerely thank Kamelah Blair and Princess Ford, from The My Black Is Whole Program, for their guidance, encouragement, and belief in my journey as a writer. Your leadership and dedication have left a lasting impact on me, not only through your individual support but also through the powerful work you both do within the mentorship organization.

To the entire team behind the mentorship program — thank you for creating a space where young voices are nurtured, challenged, and uplifted. This opportunity to write and share my story has been deeply meaningful, and it would not have been possible without the foundation you've built.

Your commitment to cultivating creativity, confidence, and purpose in emerging writers is something I will always carry with me. I'm grateful for the chance to be part of this experience, and for the door you opened that allowed this book to be written.

www.ingramcontent.com/pod-product-compliance
Lightning Source LLC
Chambersburg PA
CBHW071231160426
43196CB00012B/2487